**DO NOT REMOVE
CARDS FROM POCKET**

1/95

DOUBLE-DIP FEELINGS

Stories to Help Children Understand Emotions

by Barbara S. Cain, M.S.W.

illustrated by Anne Patterson

Gareth Stevens Publishing

MILWAUKEE

For a free catalog describing Gareth Stevens' list of high-quality books, call 1-800-341-3569 (USA) or 1-800-461-9120 (Canada).

ISBN 0-8368-0931-9

Published by

Gareth Stevens Publishing
1555 North RiverCenter Drive, Suite 201
Milwaukee, Wisconsin 53212, USA

Printed in the United States of America

1 2 3 4 5 6 7 8 9 98 97 96 95 94 93

Introduction for Parents, Teachers, and Librarians

This is a book about feelings. It is about feelings that often appear in seemingly unmatched pairs, feelings that tend to arrange themselves in confusing combinations of love and hate, joy and sadness, courage and fear.

This is a book about ambivalent feelings, "double-dip" feelings, which we frequently experience but seldom accept. Because grown-ups rarely speak openly about their own ambivalent feelings, children often struggle with these feelings alone. Some youngsters attempt to deny their feelings of anger in order to protect their feelings of love. Others question the sincerity of one feeling if its polar opposite coexists. Most children, however, have never been told that two dissimilar feelings can exist side by side at the same time.

This book presents a series of significant childhood events such as the first day of school, the birth of a sibling, or a move to a new home, and identifies two disparate feelings each event is likely to elicit. Questions are interspersed throughout the book in order to enlist children's active participation and stimulate interest in their own ambivalent emotions.

It is not expected that this book will be absorbed in one reading. Rather, it is likely that children will return to the book again and again, selecting and reselecting events and emotions that most nearly match their own at a given time—now a scene depicting loss, now envy, now fright. Hopefully, this book will encourage discussion between you and the children with whom you are in contact both at home and at school, and that the tugs and pulls of emotions can thereby become less troubling, less bewildering, and less silent.

Everyone has feelings.
There are many different kinds.

4

Sometimes we feel cheerful,
Sometimes we feel sad,
And sometimes we feel
    both cheerful *and* sad.

Sometimes we feel playful,
Sometimes we feel mad,
And sometimes we feel *both* playful *and* mad.

Did you ever have two different feelings
At the very same time?

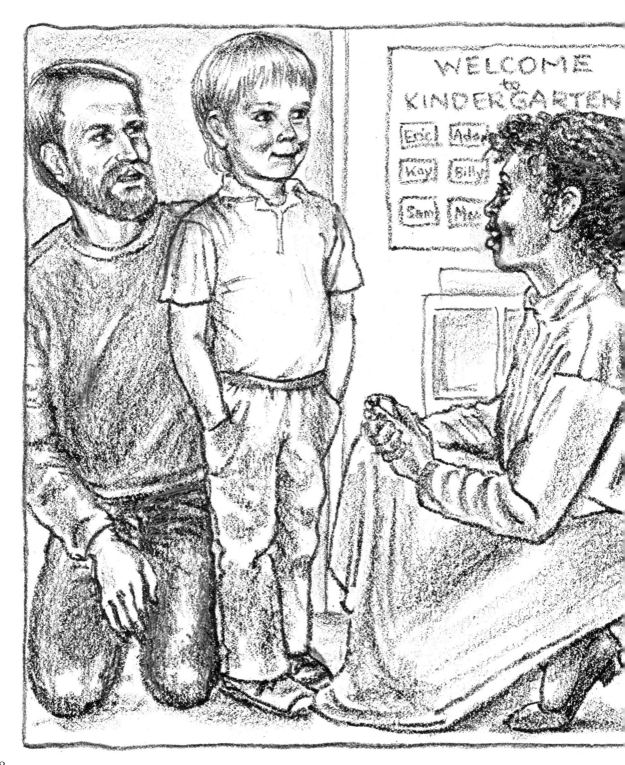

When Billy began his first day of school,
He felt big boy *proud*
And little boy *scared*.

When Amy's new brother came home to live,
She felt somersault *joy*
And left out *sad*.

When the baby painted her face with an oatmeal fist,
Amy said, "He's a funny little fellow,
And a great big pest."
Did you ever feel both *silly* and *mad*
At the very same time?

When Kathy's family moved to a different town,
She said, "I like this new house with a room of my own.
The old one was smaller, but the old one was home."
Did you ever feel both *happy* and *sad*
At the very same time?

When Dan stood on the diving board for the very first time,
He said, "I promised my Dad I would do it,
But I wish I could change my mind."
Did you ever feel both *brave* and *frightened*
At the very same time?

When classmates teased Sam for wetting his pants,
Billy said, "I'd like to tease him, too,
But he's only doing what I used to do."
Did you ever feel both *mean* and *friendly*
At the very same time?

When Dan beat Amy in the spelling bee at school,
He was *thrilled* to be a winner,
But *worried* he'd lose a friend.

When Kathy got the chicken pox and had to stay at home,
She said, "I *hate* these itchy polka dots,
But I *love* having ice cream and storybooks and Toto in bed."

When Kathy dumped her food in Toto's dish,
She was *glad* to be rid of her spinach,
But *sorry* to ruin poor Toto's lunch.

When Dan invited him for an overnight sleep,
Billy said, "I'll look silly if I bring my teddy,
But I think he'll be lonely at home by himself."
Did you ever feel both *embarrassed* and *excited*
At the very same time?

When darkness fell and it was time for bed
Amy felt *jealous* of the kids playing across the street,
But almost *happy* to go to sleep.

So, if sometimes you feel *both* happy *and* sad,
And sometimes you feel *both* sorry *and* glad,
Remember, everyone has feelings,
There are a million different kinds,
And sometimes we feel two at the very same time.

FOR MORE INFORMATION . . .

For Parents – Places to Write

Here are some places to write for more information on how to discuss different emotions with your child.

The International Child Resource
   Information Clearinghouse
1810 Hopkins
Berkeley, California 94707
[This is a clearinghouse with over 10,000 pieces of available information, so if you write, specify the exact information you would like to receive.]

Children's News
Children's Hospital and Health Center
8001 Frost Street
San Diego, California 92123

For Children – Further Reading about Emotions

Every Kid's Guide to Handling Feelings.
   Berry (Childrens Press)

Feeling Afraid. Barsuhn (Childrens Press)

Feelings, Inside You and Out Loud, Too.
   Polland (Celestial Arts)

Getting to Know Your Feelings.
   Dombrower (Heartwise)

Liking Myself. Palmer (Impact Publishers)

Sometimes I Worry. Gross
   (Childrens Press)

What are Feelings? Hazen (Forest House)

Glossary

anger: A strong feeling of displeasure toward something or someone.

embarrassment: A feeling of being nervous or self-conscious.

emotions: Feelings that people have in reaction to certain situations. It is possible to experience more than one emotion at the same time.

imagination: The mind's special ability to think of situations and characters that don't exist in real life.

jealousy: A feeling of sadness and envy. For example, you might feel jealous if your best friend decides to play with someone other than you.

Index